Contents

Introduction

Asylum seekers and refugees have become a national and regional political issue. There is a lot of confusion about them, not just about who they are but also about the impact they have on our lives. With welfare benefits, border controls and detention centres grabbing the headlines, frequently the situations of the individuals themselves are forgotten.

It happened to Me - Refugee features the stories of six young people who are at various stages of the refugee application process. They come from a variety of countries and have had different experiences, but their real-life stories give a picture of what it's really like to be an asylum seeker and a refugee. What the young people in this book have in common is a determination to survive against the odds.

What is asylum?

Asylum is the status given to people who have fled their home and travelled to another country because of persecution. Most developed countries have procedures that enable them to decide whether someone should get asylum status or not. Asylum is also called refugee status.

Who is a refugee?

The 1951 United Nations convention relating to the status of refugees defines a refugee as someone who has a well-founded fear of persecution for reasons of race, religion, nationality or membership of a social or political group. People fleeing because of famine or natural disasters are not defined by this convention as refugees, nor are people migrating simply to find a better life.

Some of the people who are interviewed in this book are not officially refugees but are asylum seekers. This means they have arrived in a country and requested asylum but that country has yet to decide whether to give them refugee status. If they are refused they will be sent home or will have the right to appeal, although the appeal process is lengthy. If they cannot prove they would be persecuted if they returned to their home country, they will not get refugee status.

Why is it such a talked-about issue?

In the year 2000 there were around 14.5 million people worldwide who were refugees or asylum seekers. Countries that have signed the 1951 convention have to consider a person's application for asylum, and look after them until a decision is made. Refugees often enter countries illegally and so there is no easy way to manage their dispersal fairly between countries. Because of this some people feel concerned about the economic burden refugees place on their country. However this concern is often unfounded as refugees can bring skills, enterprise and enthusiasm to their host country.

Where do asylum seekers come from and go to?

Asylum seekers come from all over the world. 139 countries have signed the agreement to protect genuine applicants. Only 7% of refugees go to developed countries. Most flee to neighbouring developing countries. The six people in this book fled countries in Europe, Asia and Africa. (See map below.)

Note on the interviews

The interviews are written as literally as possible from the words of the interviewee and are presented in question and answer format. At the end of each interview there are questions to discuss with friends or to help you think about the topic in more depth. The names of some of the interviewees have been changed.

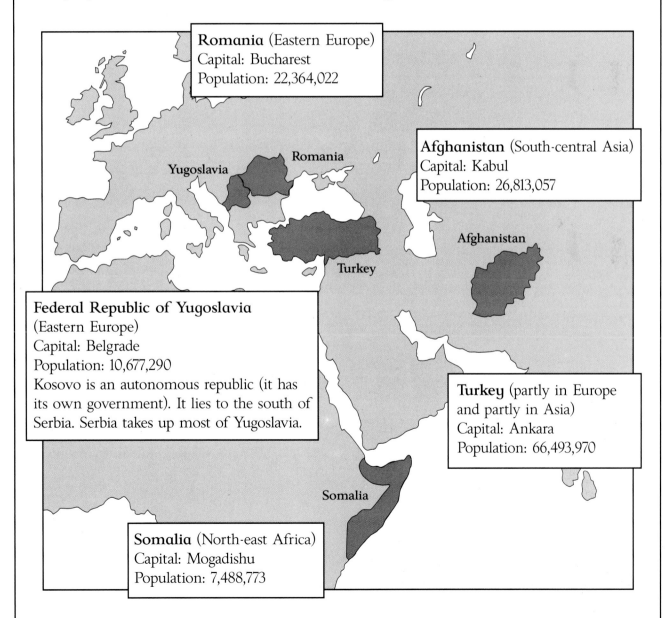

Romania (Eastern Europe)
Capital: Bucharest
Population: 22,364,022

Afghanistan (South-central Asia)
Capital: Kabul
Population: 26,813,057

Federal Republic of Yugoslavia (Eastern Europe)
Capital: Belgrade
Population: 10,677,290
Kosovo is an autonomous republic (it has its own government). It lies to the south of Serbia. Serbia takes up most of Yugoslavia.

Turkey (partly in Europe and partly in Asia)
Capital: Ankara
Population: 66,493,970

Somalia (North-east Africa)
Capital: Mogadishu
Population: 7,488,773

It Happened to Sophia*

Sophia was 17 when she travelled to the UK in early summer 2000. She intended to return to her home in Afghanistan (see opposite) after three weeks but could not. She found herself in London as an unaccompanied child asylum seeker. She was interviewed in 2001 when an international force was attempting to remove the Taliban from power in Afghanistan.

* Not her real name.

Q What was your early life in Afghanistan like?

A Both my parents are teachers - my mother taught a literacy programme for girls - and we had lots and lots of books in my house, which was quite uncommon. I could read and write before I went to nursery school. When I was six my family took me to Pakistan because they did not like the regime in power - although this was before the Taliban took over. We were there for eight years. Then the rulers in Afghanistan changed to a mujahedin government and so we went back to live in Mazar-e-Sharif [in northern Afghanistan].

Q How old were you at this time?

A It was 1996 and I was 14. I didn't want to go back because I'd heard about all the killing and horror during the Soviet War. I'd seen films of massacres, and I knew there was a civil war going on. But my father got us a house in Mazar and I went to an all-girls school connected to the university. I was very happy.

Q So what changed?

A One day I was sitting in the school when somebody came and told the teacher to leave the school. We were told just to run home. Almost immediately we started hearing rockets. When I got to the house my brother was back from school and my parents had come from work. They told us the Taliban had come into our town. We knew that they had been moving across the country because most people had satellite TV and could get the BBC and CNN. During two days the Taliban killed lots of people and took over our town. We had a basement in our house where we hid. The fighting was so fierce you could hear it all around. It was very, very frightening.

Q How did your parents react?

A Suddenly they seemed to be very bad-tempered. My father listened to all the news he could get on the radio - Voice of America, stations in Iran and Pakistan and the BBC. Our mother just tried to keep us quiet. My father got a Kalashnikov and he and my uncle, who lived with us, stayed up all night taking it in turns to be on guard.

Q How did things change in your city?

A Before, all the different tribes - Pashtuns, Hazaras, Uzbeks - mixed without thinking about it. But suddenly everyone was asking which you belonged to and what languages you spoke... people were distancing themselves from each other.

Twice the Taliban were fought off by the Northern Alliance but the third time,

Background - Afghanistan

Afghanistan is an Islamic country in southwestern Asia. For many years it fought a bitter war with the Soviet Union (USSR). When the USSR withdrew in 1989 Afghanistan was reduced to rubble. 6.2 million people, over half the world's refugee population, had fled the country. After years of fighting the USSR, and with no real government in place, Afghanistan was plunged into civil war.

In May 1996 a group of Islamic fighters called the Taliban took control of the country, ending the civil war. The Taliban, a group of ethnic Pashtuns ('talib' is a Pashtu word meaning 'religious student' or 'seeker of knowledge'), were backed by neighbouring Pakistan. Many Afghans hoped that the Taliban would bring a stability that the country had not seen for years. However, they imposed strict Islamic law, which was particularly harsh on women. A large number of Afghans fled the country and became refugees in neighbouring nations, mainly in Iran and Pakistan.

People continued to flee when Afghanistan was attacked in 2001 by international forces attempting to remove the Taliban from power.

in 1998, they took control of our area. I saw the plane take off with all the Northern Alliance leaders who had money and could escape. After that I remember the terror as the thing that filled life. Women and girls and young boys were being taken by soldiers when they went to houses. We saw a film about what happens when a town is taken over and it showed a basement full of women half dead, with their bodies cut, about to die. So my father told us all if someone comes we should kill ourselves first. It's what many people did.

Q How did your parents cope?

A I knew they were both frightened but they are strong and didn't want to show it to my brother and my younger sister and me. My mother had left work. She knew she had to do as the Taliban wanted. A neighbour bought burkas for my mother and me to wear. When we went out on the streets we saw dead bodies everywhere and the smell was terrible.

Q During this time you came to England. How did that happen?

A I didn't come as a refugee in the beginning. I had sent some of my writings to a project in the UK. They asked me to come over and help put together a book of writings about children and women's rights. I went to Pakistan with my mother, got a visa for England and caught a plane. I had people to stay with near Cambridge and I intended to stay just three weeks.

Q So why did your plans change?

A Just before I was due to return my mother phoned and said don't come back. My parents were afraid that if the Taliban discovered I had been away - they would come and punish me. That had already happened with one girl who went out of the country. I was very upset because

The Taliban forced women in Afghanistan to wear the burka.

"I took my bags to London and then went to the Home Office. There was this long queue…"

of course I wanted to go home, but I realised that my parents were trying to save me and that I must do as they said.

Q What did you do then?

A I was lucky because the people I had been staying with were able to advise me, and they let me stay until I got things sorted out. I had a visa for three months and another refugee told me how to apply for asylum. I took my bags to London and then went to the Home Office. There was this long queue and I had to wait a while and then I had to go to another floor. I was interviewed by an Indian person who asked how old I was. When I told

him he asked where I was going to stay for the night and I said I didn't know. I could see he was shocked. He gave me some addresses and said if I didn't get anything to come back. He was kind.

Q Did you get more help than this?

A I went to the Refugee Council and talked to several people. They found me a

It's a Fact that…

In Britain in 2002, 1 in 20 refugees were unaccompanied children.
In 1992 this figure was 1 in 100.

Unaccompanied children under 16 seeking asylum should be placed with foster families. Due to shortages, however, some are placed in accommodation with unassessed adults (no-one has ensured the adults are suitable to live with children).

> **" I find things I read in the papers - about refugees as scroungers and that they should be sent home - very upsetting. "**

place in a hostel and they got a taxi to take me there. Then I was given a case worker because I was under 18. She took me to the children's section of Hackney Council because a local authority has responsibility for unaccompanied child refugees who come into

their area. I was sent by them to a different hostel which was horrible. There were cockroaches and I was the only single woman - the others had families. There were hundreds of men and that didn't feel safe after the things I had known about in Afghanistan. I stayed there four months. I was given a voucher for £25 a week to look after myself. It took two months to get a decision from the Home Office giving me four years exceptional leave to remain. I know now that is quick, but I think they recognised how dangerous it was in Afghanistan.

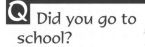 **Did you go to school?**

A No. It was the summer and schools were closed so I went to college and did summer courses - Spanish, maths, self-defence. It filled the time. Then I started studying for A levels at college in September 2000.

Q Have you experienced racism?

A Not directly but I find things I read in the papers - about refugees as scroungers and that they should be sent home - very upsetting. And one day on my politics course we were discussing immigration laws and this boy got up and was saying refugees this and that... all the stuff from the papers. But we spoke about his views in class and he really thought about it and now he's very close to me and the other refugee in class.

Q Were you in touch with your family after you came here?

A All the phone lines in Afghanistan were destroyed, and the postal system. I had no contact for a year but somehow I felt they were safe. Then my mother went to Pakistan to live with my brother and sister and she contacted me from there. We both felt I should stay here because I have a better life in Britain than I would in Pakistan.

Q And when it seemed the Taliban had been defeated and that there would be a government representative of different tribes along with UN monitoring, did you decide to return home?

A I definitely want to go back if it is safe as I miss my family very much. But I have the opportunity to get a good education here so I want to complete my studies and take something home. Also I am learning a lot about what educated women can do. I feel that will help me be strong in my own country. ■

"*I am learning a lot about what educated women can do.*"

Talking Points

◆ Sophia feels that the media represents refugees badly. How do you think the issue is handled in the press and on television?

◆ Under United Nations ruling, to gain asylum status people have to have a well-founded fear of persecution in their own country. Sophia's parents, therefore, might not be able to come to the UK if they wished. Do you think they should be allowed to keep the family together?

◆ Sophia was unhappy that the hostel she stayed in was full of men. How would you feel if you were in her place?

◆ Which of Sophia's experiences do you think would be hardest to deal with?

It Happened to Imana*

Imana, 18, travelled to the UK as an unaccompanied refugee in 2000, escaping from the war in her home country, Somalia (see opposite).

* Not her real name.

(see opposite)

Q How was your life before the war began in the early 1990s?

A I lived in Mogadishu [Somalia's capital] with my mum, dad and brothers and sisters. I went to a Muslim school. It was not an easy childhood once the war began because we knew people who were killed - my Koran [Muslim holy book] teacher was one. There was a lot of fear around. Then things got so bad that we couldn't go to school or even play in the backyard.

Q Did things get worse?

A One day in 1992 when I was nine I got home from my Koran class and found that my house had been

" Then things got so bad that we couldn't go to school or even play in the backyard. "

trashed, turned upside down with clothes lying around everywhere. My parents, brother and sisters had disappeared. I thought at first they had gone next door where my 'aunt' - that's a respectful term for an older woman who is a close friend - lived. She didn't know what had happened but said they might have escaped from Somalia and we should leave too.

Q So what did you do?

A My aunt took me to Kenya thinking we would be safe. But we were refugees there and we had to hide. The police would come and knock on doors and if you can't speak Swahili they know you are a refugee... they take you to a camp or lock you up in prison. It was a very stressful time and things that are very bad for a woman happened in that country. After two years we couldn't take it any more so we went back to Somalia.

Q Did you plan to settle there again?

A I wanted to live in Somalia but things were very bad there with the

Background - Somalia

Somalia is one of Africa's poorest countries and in recent years has suffered from drought, flooding and civil war (war between people of the same country).

Between 1969 and 1991 Somalia was ruled by Siad Barre, during which time the economy deteriorated and civil war escalated. In 1988 fighting broke out between government forces and rebel groups. Somalia, already hit by drought, became a disaster area as refugees fled and famine and disease were wide-spread. When Barre lost power, there was no organised government, as different groups fought for power. Even the United Nations could not bring about peace. By mid 1992, while rival warlords continued fighting a civil war, six million people faced starvation.

Although Somalia has no government at present, a Transitional National Government was established in October 2000. However, it is struggling to maintain a stable regime. Peace seems a long way off while civil war continues to blight the country. Lawlessness, chaos and uncertainty reign.

war. I was advised to go back to Kenya and try to find a way to get to Europe. In Kenya I worked as a maid to raise the money that I needed for a passport. People in my Islamic community were kind and gave me the last bit of money I needed.

Q Did you leave then?

A A man who organised the ticket said he would take me pretending I was his daughter. He flew with me to Heathrow but he didn't speak and said if I was questioned I should say I didn't know anything. At the airport he left me and took the passport I had paid for.

Q So there you were alone, knowing nobody. What did you do?

A I don't know what I would have done but a Somali family at the airport saw me and they were very kind. They took me to their house, gave me food and a place to sleep. I said I had an uncle in England which made them laugh. They told me it's not like Somalia where you can find people easily. Even so they did manage to get a number for him and I went to his home.

It's a Fact that...

In Australia 39% of applications for asylum for people from Somalia are approved. In the UK the figure is 48% and in the United States 60%. These figures are comparatively high because of the seriousness of the situation in Somalia.

Q Did your uncle help you?

A My uncle took me to the Home Office department to apply for asylum. I had to queue for two days to be seen. He offered to let me stay with him but I couldn't. He was a man on his own living in a place with one bedroom and at night all his men friends would visit. I was scared of what would happen to me. So I told him I had somewhere to go.

Q Did you get help to find somewhere to stay?

A I went to social services and they sent me to a place in Croydon. When the woman in charge opened the door there was someone else's stuff in the room and you could smell shoes, aftershave.... but I didn't complain. I just started cleaning up. Then about four in the morning the door burst open and there was this drunk guy with his friends telling me to get out. I ran downstairs and next

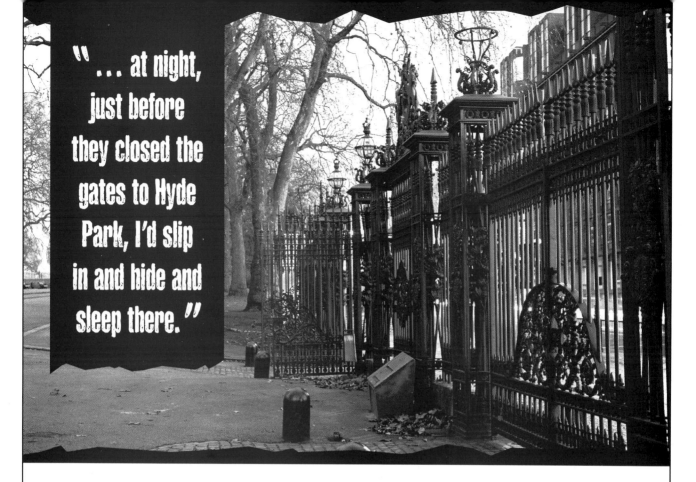

" ... at night, just before they closed the gates to Hyde Park, I'd slip in and hide and sleep there. "

day I went back to social services. They said they had given me a place and couldn't help any more. In the end they did but I was moved from place to place.

Q What happened to your request for asylum during this time?

A I was given indefinite leave to remain (ILR) this year which was a big relief and made me happy. But then I was thrown out of the place I was living because it was a hostel for asylum seekers and I wasn't a seeker any more.

Q What did you do then?

A I wasn't given another place to stay so I spent days walking around Oxford Circus and then at night, just before they closed the gates to Hyde Park, I'd slip in and hide and sleep there. I did that for six nights then one of the friends I met also sleeping there told me about walk-in centres for the homeless where I could get something to eat. From going there I heard about Centrepoint and they agreed to let me stay there. I got clothes from their donation

centre. One way and another it was just possible to manage and the people at Centrepoint helped me get benefits sorted out.

Q Did you have any education?

A For a while I was staying in Swiss Cottage and the manageress of the house gave me, and other refugee kids there, brochures and addresses of a college we could go to. My English wasn't very good but my teacher was nice and helped. Even so I found it very hard because I couldn't keep up with the other

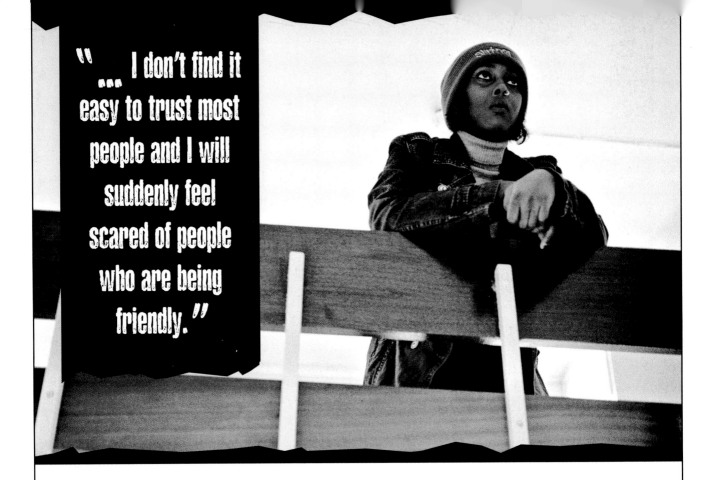

> " ... I don't find it easy to trust most people and I will suddenly feel scared of people who are being friendly. "

students and they were rude. I felt everyone was talking about me. I was trying to do an NVQ in computers but then I was moved again so I had to leave. Now I'm waiting to be settled before I start college again.

Q So what do you do with your time?

It's a Fact that...

Iraq, Sri Lanka, Federal Republic of Yugoslavia, Iran, Somalia and Afghanistan accounted for about half of UK asylum applications in 2000. Serious human rights abuses occur in all of these countries, including torture.

A I go to the Medical Foundation for Victims of Torture where I am supposed to see my counsellor, Sheila, twice a week and there I talk to her about things that sometimes I imagine... what has happened to my family... soldiers coming to the house... things that happened to me in Kenya that make me ashamed... she is very good for me. I was sent there because they help young people who they think are suffering from traumatic situations and conflict. There are also groups for people like me twice a week and I go to those. I have met other Somalis through the groups and I get along with them.

> ## "I don't feel love for any country because I don't feel I belong anywhere."

But I don't find it easy to trust most people and I will suddenly feel scared of people who are being friendly.

Q Are there things you do by yourself that you enjoy?

A I go to the library and draw a lot. I like art and I have been told I am good at it. One of the social services ladies gave me a nice box of crayons.

Q Now you are eighteen you get adult benefits. Can you manage on that?

A I get £84 every two weeks and I find it hard to manage. I pay £17 for rent and transport costs £20. I am given bread, milk and tea for breakfast and a good dinner where I live. Even so there is not much money for other food or clothes and I do find it very cold in England.

Q What are your feelings about Somalia now?

A I don't feel love for Somalia or Kenya. I don't feel love for any country because I don't feel I belong anywhere. But I do miss my 'aunt' and I write to her sometimes. I don't know if she gets the letters. I wouldn't want to move from London now because at least I don't have to hide here and I do have some friends. One in particular - a girl from Ethiopia who understands how I feel.

Q What would make you feel happy here?

A The thing I most want is to have a place of my own. I don't like being in a sharing house. At night there are always noises and I am scared. I take sleeping pills every night.

Q Do you ever talk about your parents?

A When people ask I tell them I don't have a mum or dad. It's easier than trying to explain. But sometimes I think that if I was able to get here by myself perhaps they managed to escape and are somewhere in the world. I like to believe that because it gives me hope. ∎

Talking Points

◆ Imana was only nine when her family disappeared and she has had many different experiences. What qualities do you think she possesses to have made it through all that?

◆ Imana doesn't feel she belongs anywhere. Do you think it's important to feel you 'belong' to a particular country? How would you feel if you were in her position?

It Happened to Vlad

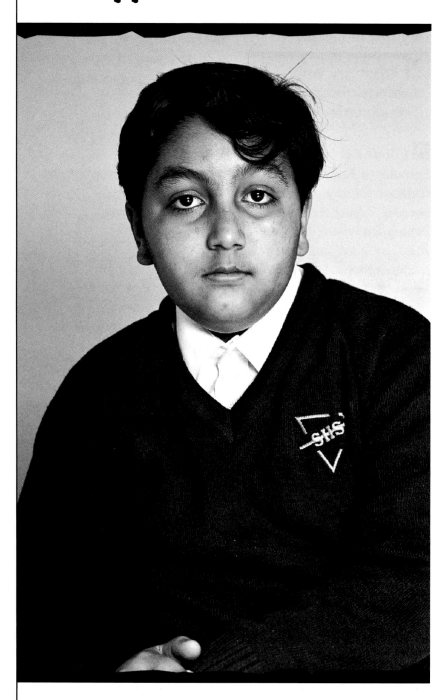

Vlad, 11, and his mother Florina fled to the UK from their home town of Ciurari, Romania (see opposite) in 2000. They now have full refugee status and live in Croydon.

Q How was Romania before you left?

A The discrimination against Roma people was very bad. When there was still communism the hatred was there but it was harder for people to act on. But since the fall of communism [1989] and 'democracy' has come in nobody stops people like the Nationalists from attacking Roma people. People around us, whom we knew, were being attacked and killed and the police did nothing.

Q How bad did it get?

A My uncle's house was set fire to when someone put a Molotov cocktail through the door. [Vlad's uncle and father were in the house.] The police pretended they would help my uncle... but when he came out they put handcuffs on him and told the Romanian people that they were free to kill him. It sounds crazy to say it over here but in Romania politicians are telling the ordinary non-Roma people that they can kill us, because we do not belong in the country. When my

Background - Romania

Romania is in southeastern Europe. Ethnic Romanians make up about 89% of the population. The largest minority groups are Hungarians (7% of the population), Roma (or Gypsies) (2% of the population) and Germans (less than 1% of the population).

Since the end of communist rule in 1989, the Roma people have been a target of harassment and hostility. In the early 1990s a large number of Roma left Romania for Germany, but the German government sent many of them back the following year.

Anti-Roma protests have increased across Eastern Europe since the early 1990s. Romani peoples in Western Europe are also under pressure to abandon their traditional nomadic way of life. In France, for example, their access to campsites has been restricted.

father came out, the house was burning and the police grabbed my father and pushed him in. Later my mother found his legs. She went to the town prosecutor but he did nothing.

Q Where was your mother when this happened?

A She was at the house of another brother. When she heard she ran home and she saw the police and the people marching around saying they were looking for Romas to kill.

Q What did you do then?

A My mother was very very upset but she told me it was too dangerous to stay and that we must go that night. We walked 20 kilometres to another village. We found an apartment but even there it felt menacing on the street. My mother felt particularly at risk because she had been working on human rights issues. Several times the police had gone through her papers in her office.

"People around us, whom we knew, were being attacked and killed and the police did nothing."

19

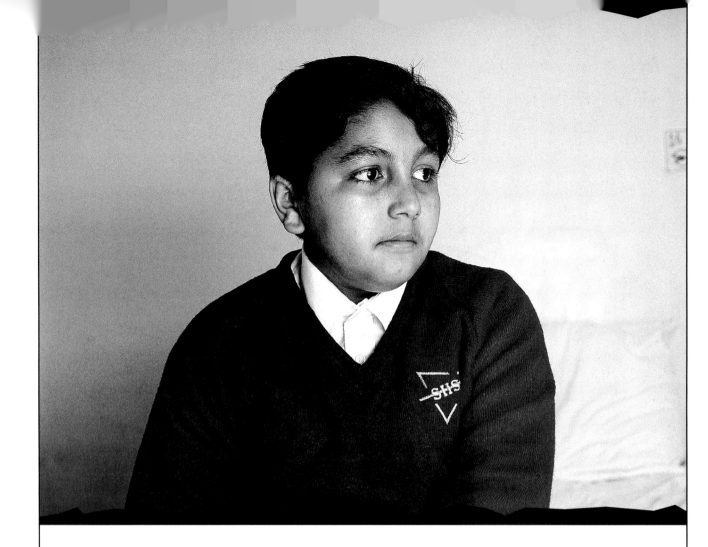

Q Were you safe then?

A We weren't safe because the police found us and broke into our apartment in the early hours of the morning. They came into the room with big dogs and they pulled the duvet off my bed. I felt they had all the strength and nobody could protect us. They were shouting at my mother and that upset me a lot. They told her she had an hour to get out.

Q What did you do?

A When they had gone my mother said we must go at once. I knew she was right because I felt frightened all the time. I had thought for a long time that they would come and kill us one day. We just grabbed our clothes and things. My mother told me to be very quiet while we were getting out. She had managed to arrange a car which was waiting outside the flat and it took us to the train station. We caught a train to Hungary and I remember feeling so relieved when we had got out of Romania. We stayed in Hungary for a while. But our plan was to go to England. Because my mother had some money she was able to buy a ticket to travel there. We went all the way by train.

Q How did you manage when you arrived?

A In Hungary my mum organised to be a student and do a course in Brighton. It

> **" I knew that as a Roma I would never be helped to get into university but here that can happen. "**

was very nice because a host family had been arranged, I think through the college, and they had us to stay with them in Brighton. They were so friendly and it was a really good first impression of England. My mother became good friends with the wife and even though we didn't stay long we still go and visit them.

Q What did you do in Brighton?

A I went to school there for three weeks and I enjoyed it very much. It was a surprise for me to find that it didn't seem to matter what colour children were. I also did extra classes in English at a special college, after school

hours, because I needed to learn the language quickly.

Q Did you stay in Brighton?

A We didn't stay in Brighton long. For some reason my mum's studies there didn't work out and we moved to London. We had applied for asylum and we were given a place in a hostel in North London. My mother went to study at North London University for a while but they couldn't find a school place for me there so two months ago we were moved to another hostel near Croydon.

Q Do you go to school there?

A I am in a school and I like it a lot. The teachers tell me I am doing well and

already I have some certificates. In Romania I was always frightened in school because of the bullying and because they were very mean to me. When I went all the time and did better with my work than other children, the teacher just marked me absent. I knew that as a Roma I would never be helped to get into university but here that can happen. The thing that pleases my mum is that I come home from school full of enthusiasm and I have opinions. She says it was never like that in our country.

Q Do you have friends here?

A I have made friends quite easily in school. The children seemed interested

It's a Fact that...

About 24% of asylum applications are successful in the UK. In Australia the figure is 23%. If someone is given refugee status it means they can live and work in a country without any restrictions.

"I love my mother but I don't want to live in the same room."

VICTORY IS MINE

in knowing about me. I tried to tell them about my experiences. It is still difficult for me to explain things properly in English. But I don't spend time with them out of school.

Q So what do you do in your free time?

A I spend most of the free time with my mother.

Sometimes we go to the park and she might play football with me, but she is not very good. Or we go to the swimming pool. On Sundays we go to church in Dulwich. We spend a lot of time in our room and we play cards and invent games. We talk about everything. It's part of our tradition in Romania for parents to discuss everything with children.

Q How is your housing?

A We have one very small room and share a kitchen with a lot of other people. My mother and I sleep side by side on two beds but there is not much room for anything else in the room besides a small table and the TV. Sometimes we have disagreements and she tells me how I should behave. I love my mother but I don't want to live in the same room. In Romania I had my own room.

Q Will you be offered a bigger home?

A We have been offered another place but my mother doesn't want to go because she knows the building and it has been broken in to. She says she is too frightened to move there because of the things that happened in Romania, and it is very dangerous when somebody breaks in. She says there are

a lot of drugs and alcohol there and that worries her for me. Her case worker doesn't seem to understand... I see my mother crying and I just want the housing people to understand and give her a safe house. My mother says if she is told she has to go there she will sleep on the streets.

Q Do you manage on the benefits you get?

A We manage but it's hard always watching every bit of money. We eat very simply and just occasionally have fish and chips as a real treat. I have to wear second-hand and cheap clothes and sometimes I complain but my mother tells me not to worry her about it.

Q So do you ever wish you were living back in Romania?

A I never want to go back. I still have nightmares sometimes about what happened. I think of England as my country now. My mother is so happy that she has refugee status and she very much wants to study more and get a job to earn money but also as an example to me. She says I am a sacrificed child with no father to protect me and she feels God has given us a chance to find a better life here. On the wall is a poster that says 'Victory is Mine - Defeat is for My Enemy' and that is how she sees things. We can and will win by settling here and doing well.

Talking Points

◆ Vlad is happy and settled in England. However, his home country is Romania. If the situation in Romania improves and it is safe for Vlad and his mother to go back, should they have to go back even if they don't want to?

◆ What do you think of Vlad's mother's attitude to moving to a different home?

It Happened to Mira*

Mira, 14, came to the UK with both her father, a carpenter, and her mother, a meat technician, in May 1999 when she was 11. They were forcibly expelled from Kosovo (see opposite) by the Serbs and sent to a refugee camp in Albania. They paid a man they refer to as a racketeer to buy passports and tickets so they could get into the UK. They have been given leave to stay in the UK for a year but must appeal to stay longer after that.

* Not her real name.

Q What was your life like before you had to leave?

A I was born in Pristina and I grew up with Kosovan Albanian friends. We all went to school together. I was happy and I didn't think things could go wrong.

Q How much did things change then?

A The war in Kosovo started in 1998 when the Serbs began to order people out of the country. My mother told me how Milosevic was killing Kosovans. Then NATO began bombing and my parents were very frightened about what was going to happen to us. There was violent fighting in the streets in Pristina and there were problems for me getting to school. I saw terrible things on TV. We knew people were being ordered to go by the Serbian police. Then they came to our house and said, 'You don't belong here. Your country is Albania.' They gave us three hours to get our things together and leave. I didn't really understand what was happening because my parents tried not to worry me, but they just said we had to go.

A I asked if we really had to and they said yes, we couldn't risk staying. I thought of all the things I would have to leave, like my granny who I love very much - we slept in the same room in our home in Kosovo and she used to read me stories. She was very special to me. And my auntie and my cousins are still there and all my friends and even the chickens and the cat. I don't have any brothers or sisters so I couldn't share what was happening with anyone.

Q What did you do then?

A I took just the things I really needed and a book of Shakespeare's plays which are special to me, but I wasn't able to take toys. Then we were put on a bus with a lot of other people to go to Albania, which was a three-hour journey. Nobody spoke on the bus because the armed police were there and we were all very scared. In fact my mother told me later we had been lucky because the bus-load before had a terrible time. The men were separated from the women and children and killed.

Background - Kosovo

Kosovo is an area in southwestern Serbia, in the Federal Republic of Yugoslavia.

Kosovo was fairly independent of Serbia until conflict arose between the Kosovan Albanians (who make up 75% of the population) and Serbs. In 1990 the Serbian government abolished Kosovo's parliament. So in the mid-1990s some ethnic Albanians tried to gain independence for Kosovo. In the fighting that resulted hundreds of people were killed and more than 200,000 were driven from their homes – most of them were ethnic Albanians.

Despite intervention from the North Atlantic Treaty Organisation (NATO), crimes against ethnic Albanians continued, with Serbian police and the Yugoslav army destroying villages and forcing residents to flee. The United Nations (UN) estimated that nearly 640,000 people were forced out of Kosovo between March 1998 and the end of April 1999. Most of the refugees went to Albania, the former Yugoslav Republic of Macedonia, or Montenegro.

In June 1999 a peace plan for Kosovo was finally agreed. NATO-led peacekeeping forces were brought in to keep order and to ensure the safe return of Kosovan refugees, who numbered about 780,000 by the time the peace agreement was reached.

Q When you reached Albania what happened?

A We got out and there was a big stadium with lots of people from Kosovo in it. Some were crying. It was very big and I felt confused, but we were given food there and we were given a place to sleep in the football stadium in a place with lots of beds. I just knew I had to stay close to my mum and dad all the time. My mum was sad and I knew I had to be strong and look after her a bit. My dad was sad too but he didn't want to show it.

Q When did you leave the camp?

A We stayed about two weeks. We wanted to come to England as asylum seekers but we had no passports. Then we met this man who said he could get us passports and tickets to travel. It cost my parents almost all their savings - $10,000 (US) but at least the man gave my parents good advice about what to do when we got to England. Afterwards my mum felt upset that they had to give everything because she didn't know how we would manage once we reached England. We took a taxi to the airport to fly first to Greece, then to France and then we went with the train to England. My mum spent $2000 (US) on clothes for us in Albania because she had been advised to look smart when we arrived in England.

Q How was the journey?

A On the train from France to London my mum was terrified. We had been told not to speak in any language in case we were stopped. We all knew what we were doing was illegal and we have never lived that way before. My mum hates the term 'asylum seeker' because she feels the fight to be accepted has meant losing dignity.

Q What happened when you arrived in England?

A We claimed asylum immediately we arrived in the country so we were what is known as Port Applicants and it meant we were entitled to benefits. If we had waited even a day we would have been in-country applicants and things are not so simple then. We reached Waterloo

about 4 p.m. I remember it was very cold and intimidating. We were directed to the place where the Home Office officials see asylum seekers and a very nice woman interviewed us. She seemed to understand that we all felt scared but she got us an interpreter which helped. My mother had some money in her bag and she asked the Home Office woman if she wanted it. But she said, 'No. It's yours. Hide it!'

"My mum hates the term 'asylum seeker' because she feels the fight to be accepted has meant losing dignity."

Q What happened in your first days?

A We were given a hotel place for one night. The next morning we went to the DSS and they gave us benefits. We receive 70% of it in vouchers and £10 in cash and child benefit. I remember just looking at everything, seeing big buildings and I remember thinking them very tall and old and beautiful. But then it hit me we were in England and we were going to be staying here. I didn't understand anything because I didn't speak any English and at that moment I just wished I could be home and safe in my country.

Q Where did you stay after your first night?

A We went to a hotel in Queen's Park where we had a room with a shower built in and that was where we lived. The kitchen was separate and shared with another family. We all felt very lost and wondered what our life here would be like. And because my parents didn't speak much English then it wasn't easy for them. We stayed there about 13 months and then a letter came offering us a flat. When I first saw it I was so delighted because I had my own room and I'd never had that before.

> **"We all felt very lost and wondered what our life here would be like."**

Q Did you go to school?

A We were very lucky because Salusbury Primary School was very near our hotel so I was able to go there. We were told that the children of all asylum seekers are entitled to a school place but this was a special school because attached to it is the Salusbury World Centre which gives all kinds of support to refugee children. The woman who runs it, Nina, really made me feel welcome when we visited the school. We filled in forms and I was able to start two weeks later. When I got there on the first day Nina had found an Albanian pupil, Ardita, in my class and she said I could go around with her and, as she spoke English, she could interpret for me.

Q How did you cope being in school in a strange country?

A It felt strange because the school was so big and I only spoke a few words of English. The first month I felt very lost and

It's a Fact that...

In early 2002 there were 74,000 asylum seekers in Britain, 24,000 with outstanding applications and 50,000 appealing against refused applications. About 40% come from Europe, mainly the former Yugoslavia and Turkey, 33% come from Sri Lanka, India and the Middle East, the remainder come from African countries such as Somalia and Ethiopa.

I didn't seem to be learning anything. Sometimes when I went home I started crying remembering my life and my friends at home. But Nina introduced me to other children who were in a similar situation to mine and that was comforting. I worked very hard to learn English because I knew I couldn't make many friends until I could speak to them. Sometimes I would ask the girl who spoke my language to help me say things to other children but she wasn't always there. So I spent a lot of time just being quiet and alone.

> **"I worked very hard to learn English because I knew I couldn't make many friends until I could speak to them."**

Q Were the children interested in your life in Kosovo?

A They didn't ask and I didn't want to talk about it.

I wanted to be part of life in England. The thing that helped me was being involved in a school play that grew out of workshops about the experience of coming to a new country.

Q Now you've been in school - first primary and now secondary school - for three years do you feel the same as the other children?

A Sometimes I feel I am more grown-up because of what I have been through. Other children don't do as much work as I do, but I feel driven because I want to make something of my life here and please my parents. I have been getting very good marks and there are children who call me 'goody goody'. I don't want to be seen like that so I say things like, 'Yes but I've been given a detention...'

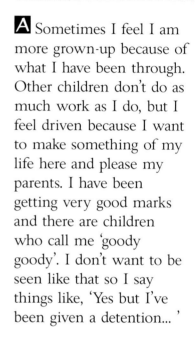

" Sometimes I feel I am more grown-up because of what I have been through. "

> ## "[My mother] feels as though she is fighting another war just to be allowed to lead an ordinary life."

Q Do you have good friends in England?

A I have one friend from Pristina and sometimes I go to her house to play. Once a month she comes to see me. But I don't have many friends and sometimes I'm a bit lonely. I would like more friends. I haven't been to a birthday party yet. Sometimes I think it's because I'm different. So I spend a lot of time reading and on Saturdays I mostly watch TV or go out for a walk. My mother has an elderly woman friend who is really kind and invites us to tea and takes us to the theatre and cinema. The other day we went to see a film together.

Q So will you stay in England?

A We want to stay although I would like to be able to go back and see my friends in Kosovo when it's really safe. My parents are just settling in and both of them go to classes to increase their education, but it's not certain we will be allowed to.

In March the year after we had come here we were refused asylum but Salusbury School was wonderful and supported us in going for an appeal.

They set up a campaign, held meetings and several classes from the school wrote letters. They rounded up support from the head teacher, school trustees, solicitors, Save the Children and other organisations. The result was that we were given an extra year to stay. But of course we have to go through another appeal after that and my mother finds the strain very hard. She sometimes says she feels as though she is fighting another war just to be allowed to lead an ordinary life. ■

Talking Points

◆ Mira was very disorientated when she came to the UK. What sort of things do you think can be done to help children like her?

◆ Mira's mother feels she is fighting another war just to stay in the UK. Why do you think it is so difficult to gain refugee status?

◆ Mira has no brothers or sisters and felt she couldn't share her experience with any one. How do you think that feels? What could she have done to help herself? Who do you share major experiences with?

It Happened to Blauden

Blauden,12, arrived in the UK from Kosovo (see page 25) with his mother and brother Bernard, 10, in June 1999. They have leave to remain until 2002.

Q What was your life in your village of Gjakova like before the war?

A We led a simple life. My father ran a little shop selling small items. We did not have much money but it was a happy time for me. I felt safe and carefree.

Q Why did you leave Kosovo?

A My mother had been threatened by the Serbian army that they would kill my brother and me if she didn't tell where my father was. He had left the year before to join the Kosovo Liberation Army and he was in hiding. She didn't tell this to my brother and me because she didn't want to frighten us. Then one day she just said we had to go. It was the right thing to do because later, when I was in England, I saw on the television news that the Serbian Army were in Gjakova and there were many dead bodies found on the streets.

Q What was leaving like?

A We left at night very quickly with other people

from the village. We were wearing just our pyjamas and we didn't have shoes and socks. We walked over the mountains to Albania which took two days. For two nights we slept in the open air. It was very cold and there were not enough blankets.

Q What happened when you reached Albania?

A I don't remember much about the camp where we waited before travelling except that food was rationed and there were a lot of tents made of canvas and each family had one of these. Inside ours there was a cooker, a carpet and three beds. We stayed several months and I made friends with other children.

Q Did you see your father before you left?

A We didn't see him in Kosovo but he came to see us in the camp for just a few hours. He brought money for my mother and said, 'Take this and look after yourselves. Buy something for Blauden and Bernard. Goodbye. We will meet again sometime'. Then he was gone and I haven't seen him since.

Q How did you get to England?

A My mother paid $5000 (US) to someone who got us tickets to travel to England. We took a boat from Albania to Italy which took ten days. It was not very safe and my mother was worried. Two people died on the boat which was very crowded. But we had no choice because we would have died for certain if we had stayed in Kosovo. We then got a train to France and then one to England.

Q How did you feel about leaving your country and going somewhere you did not know?

A I was sad to leave my place and friends but in a way we were looking forward to going to London. We had heard a lot about England and we thought it would be a good place to go to. At Waterloo I was amazed to see the escalators. Then a policeman pointed us to where people wanting asylum have to go for help. A woman who spoke

33

" At Waterloo I was amazed to see the escalators. "

Kosovan interviewed us and told us what we had to do if we wanted to try to stay. My mother told her she had the telephone number of a friend and we rang but nobody came to pick us up and so we slept for one night in the underground station.

Q What did you do after this?

A We were sitting on the street next day when someone from Kosovo saw us and was very kind and took us to their home for the night. Next day the husband took us to Hackney and a very kind woman there, who was helping refugees, found us a room to live in. It is just one room but warm and just fine for us. Then she helped us sort out benefits so we got a book of vouchers for food. We were given forms to apply for asylum but we couldn't understand them... that upset my mother. But then the kind woman found us a solicitor who spoke Kosovan.

Q What happened then?

A It's not very clear in my mind but we went to different places and saw lots of people. I got quite sick and my mother took me to a doctor. I was given medicines for my cough. We stayed indoors a lot.

I felt very alone and lost, as though I didn't belong anywhere.

Q Did you go to school?

A When the schools went back in September I was given a place at Hungerford Primary School and then everything changed. On the first day the head introduced me but I was a bit shy because I felt different to other children. I thought they would laugh at me but they were kind and helped me and very polite. One day the second strongest boy in the school suggested we play football and that helped me to be popular. And it wasn't too difficult with other subjects because the teachers always stopped and explained things. I was very happy to be at this school. My brother is at the same school.

Q How did you manage learning English?

A My teacher was Mr Hogan and he helped by giving me a dictionary in Albanian and English. At home in the evenings all the family used it and we tested each other on words. Because I was mixing with

It's a Fact that...

UK Home Office research shows that people born outside the UK (including refugees and asylum seekers) are significant contributors to the economy. It is estimated that they pay 10% more into the Treasury than they take out.

"I was very happy to be at this school."

It's a Fact that...

As Europe tightens immigration controls, it has now become virtually impossible for someone fleeing persecution to reach safety in the UK legally.

children speaking English all the time my language developed quickly and I worked hard to learn all the spellings every week. It was more difficult for my mother. I still have to help her a bit although she is going to college to study English. In fact I learned so much that I wrote a story about coming to England as a refugee called, 'A New Life in England'. The school entered it for the Cambridge Young Writers' Award and I was a runner up and my story was published in a book.

Q Do you think about your father much?

A In the beginning when I went to school children asked where my dad was and that made me very sad. Other children saw I was sad and told them to leave me alone. I try to make myself think I don't have a father because it is upsetting to remember too much.

Q Do you have many friends?

A I have good friends at school but my mother doesn't allow me to go to other children's houses. She says it's because she doesn't know the parents properly. And when there was a school trip and my friends were going my mum wouldn't let me go. She's scared to have me away in a situation she doesn't know very well because she still feels frightened. In my country things happened to children when they were away from their homes. Even though I am at secondary school now she still takes me and collects me. I do understand how she feels so I wasn't cross even though I would have liked to go.

Q What do you do with your time when you are not at school?

A In the evenings and at weekends I do homework and watch TV, so does my brother. My mother does housework. Then we go to the park sometimes, or perhaps to the shops. We sometimes go to the cinema. We have met two local families who are Kosovan and they have children. They visit us sometimes.

Q Do you want to go back to Kosovo?

A I would like to see my dad again and my friends there. But I don't really want to go back. I still have nightmares about what happened there and it's not safe even now. Many of my friends have died, for example one was playing and a bomb placed under the ground exploded. It would also be hard for all of us after the freedom we have here. We can go everywhere and people are kind to us and make us feel welcome. I tell you I have really found the peace that I was looking for here in England. ■

Talking Points

◆ Blauden's mother is cautious about what she allows him to do. Do you think she is right to be cautious? What effect do you think this might have on Blauden?

◆ Often children adapt to new countries faster than their parents. Why do you think this is? Is it easier for children to move to another country or not?

It Happened to Tarik*

Two years ago Tarik fled to Australia seeking asylum after being involved with human rights organisations in Turkey (see opposite). He lives with two other men at the back of a shop in Melbourne's inner city area. He is shy speaking English and speaks very softly although his English is excellent. The photographs of him have been altered because he fears he would be identified if he ever went back to Turkey.

* Not his real name.

Q How old were you when you came to Australia?

A I was 25. That was two years ago.

Q Were you working in Turkey?

A Yes, I was working in a bank as an officer. I had been working there for three years. I have also worked for human rights organisations.

Q Why did you flee Turkey?

A I was part of a leftist group, the Turkish Communist Workers Party. Although Turkey says it is democratic, it is not. They don't like any activity that criticises the government.

Q What do you mean by not being democratic?

A Well, you see, here in Australia you can say what you think. But in my country if you say what you think about the system and are against them in your beliefs you can have trouble. For example although I am Turkish, I have many Kurdish friends. I do not feel it is right that they cannot speak their own language in Turkey. They do not have that right. People should be able to speak their own language.

Q What upsets you about the government so much that you will put your life on the line like this?

A It is a matter of beliefs. I believe in a socialist system where everything is more equally divided between people. If you go along with what the government wants Turkey is an easy country to live in. Most people are happy to do this.

Q Why were you picked up and put in prison?

A I was selling newspapers at the main station in Istanbul, the central station. The government don't like newspapers that question their behaviour. They don't like opposition which I think is what a democracy means.

Background - Turkey

Turkey is situated in southeastern Europe and southwestern Asia. It has a population of 66.6 million, which is around 80% Turkish and 20% Kurdish.

The human rights organisation Amnesty International has reported that in Turkey writers, politicians, religious leaders, human rights defenders and many others have been tried and imprisoned for exercising their right to freedom of expression, particularly for expressing opinions on the treatment of Kurds or the role of Islam. In 2000 there were numerous reports of torture and ill-treatment of men, women and children. Many of the victims were political activists, including supporters of leftist, pro-Kurdish and Islamic groups. Other victims of torture and ill-treatment included Kurdish villagers, relatives of political activists, students and members of women's groups.

The authorities are reluctant to investigate allegations of torture. Medical evidence is frequently withheld and the intimidation of witnesses and a climate of fear also prevent investigation.

In December 1997 the European Union (EU) denied Turkey's application for full membership, as it cannot be accepted while it continues to violate human rights.

Q How long were you in prison?

A I was there for seven days but I was tortured a lot.

Q Is it normal for the police to torture prisoners?

A They are working like a machine. And they don't need to use guns, they have another type of torture. They make people go crazy by putting them in completely white rooms with the light on all the time and unable to hear anything. You can go blind like this. The rooms are only very small, two metres by two metres, so they cannot move as well. Can you imagine this? Or they play loud music 24 hours a day. This also makes people crazy because there is no escape. So you don't always need guns to torture people.

> " ... you don't always need guns to torture people. "

There was a hunger strike amongst the prisoners in Turkey recently and nearly a hundred people died. They were imprisoned because of their beliefs. I would be with them on a hunger strike if I had not been able to come to Australia. They are there only for their political beliefs.

Q So how did you come to Australia?

A I came in a hurry because my case had not been finished in the courts in Turkey. My friends and parents helped me get a passport very quickly and bought me a ticket for Australia. I also had a visa to visit. I came by plane. I was frightened at the airport in

Turkey that I would be on the computer records of people who are wanted by the police. But I was lucky because my case had not yet finished and I was not on the missing list. I am now. I have an uncle who came here some years ago and he now lives here with his family. It was very expensive to leave Turkey like this but my parents have paid back, slowly, every bit of the money it cost.

Q Tell me about your uncle.

A He is my mother's brother and he is also a refugee. He was imprisoned for four and a half years because he was working for

It's a Fact that...

Refugees in Australia are entitled to 510 hours of free English language instruction which must be taken in the first two years.

Australia is one of the most difficult countries in the world to get to. It has no common borders and there are universal visa requirements. Because of this it is highly unlikely that it will ever see the large numbers of asylum seekers other countries experience.

a human rights centre in Turkey. I remember visiting him in jail in Turkey when I was younger and I was terribly upset because he was covered in blood. His shirt was all bloody. It made a deep impression on me that a man could be treated like this. He is now working in Australia as an electronic technician.

Q What happened when you first arrived?

A It was awful for me because I had no concept of a future. The future was empty. Nothing was there. I could not see anything in the weeks ahead of me. And I also had to talk to the authorities about why I was here and what had happened and without language it was so hard.

Q What's it like to rely on a translator?

A So very hard, even in translation you are still not sure what is being said, you see. If it is all as you mean it to be. And having to talk about it all the time was not good for me. At times I started to cry when I remember. If you tell your story all the time you live it again.

Q What were the most difficult things for you initially?

A Not having language complicates things in every way. When I came I didn't know any English at all. It was very hard. I lived with my uncle and his family and they were the only people I could talk with because they spoke my language. I went to school - to learn English - but I couldn't concentrate because I was thinking about my case [seeking asylum as a political refugee] all the time. My first application seeking refuge in Australia was rejected because of problems with the translation. I was very, very worried about my future. I was so worried about them sending me back. This problem with getting the right visa has always made me very anxious. It has caused a lot of trouble and has also cost much money to my friends and parents.

" I remember visiting [my uncle] in jail in Turkey when I was younger and I was terribly upset because he was covered in blood."

Q How do you manage financially here?

A I was not allowed to work because of my status but some organisations - Red Cross, Brotherhood of St Laurence, Refugee Centre - and some others have helped me with things like beds and food. I am learning to do some ceramic work, which will help me pay for things when I am studying.

Q How is the way of life different from here and Turkey?

A Well for me, because I can't talk English very well I am always embarrassed to talk to people so I don't have enough friends. I miss my friends all the time because everyone needs friends to talk to. I think how I lived through the earthquake a few years ago and they are waiting for another to happen. So I am always thinking of what if there is another earthquake something might happen to my parents and friends. I am so far away and cannot help them. But I would have to return then. I couldn't stay if something happened to them.

Q Are you working at all at the moment?

A I can't work until my English is better and I can talk to people comfortably You see the language is such a big problem. I am a shy person.

Q Who do you live with now?

A One Turkish man, Hassan, who owns the house and one other man. Hassan is teaching me the ceramic work. They are like brothers to me. I can share my feelings with them.

Q What do you most like about Australia?

A It's better than Turkey for me because I feel safe. With a permanent residence I feel safe. It is very nice to go

42

It's a Fact that....

The world's poorest countries bear by far the greatest 'asylum strain' – if you compare numbers of refugees with the host country's national wealth.

The vast majority of refugees go to neighbouring countries. Iran currently hosts 1.8 million refugees from Afghanistan; Pakistan has 1.2 million.

outside, to walk around and always feel safe and relaxed. I also feel I can get an education here because the government helps you. In Turkey I wanted to go to university to study but it is too expensive.

Q But would you still like to be in Turkey?

A Of course! It is my country and it is a very nice country. A very beautiful and alive country. I just don't like the system. I see it is very unjust.

Q What would happen if you went back to Turkey?

A I would be sent to prison. I came here before my case was finished so they are looking for me still. I am very lucky to be here, lucky to leave there.

Q So you cannot return to your country until the government changes?

A No. If I get an Australian passport, which is what I am in the process of doing now, I might be able to return. I have been accepted as a genuine refugee and I have to wait for just one more year and I will have a passport. Then I can go back to visit my parents.

Q Are your family politically active?

A No. They are sympathetic to ideals but not politically active.

Q Do you think your parents would like to come here?

A They would like it here because I am here! You know how parents feel about their children.

Q Can your parents visit you?

A Apart from the cost it is difficult because the Australian government might not believe they will return to Turkey - they might not want to give them a visa. But I can apply for them to come to live here eventually. It will take at least five years with all the bureaucracy and the waiting queues.

Q How do you feel about being so far away?

A I am very worried about them all the time. I love my family. Because I ran away from the police, they will be asking my parents about me so I can't contact them openly. I can telephone them sometimes but I don't have enough money to call all the time. I feel alone here because not only do my parents live in Turkey but all my friends and relatives as well.

Q Emotionally and physically are you very different from the person you were in Turkey?

A I feel tired all the time now. Not just because it is all very emotionally tiring to have anxiety about the visa and my safety and status - but because I was tortured in prison I have a lot of pain as a result. I was beaten up constantly and tied in bad positions. Bones were broken in different parts of my body and I still suffer pain from the injuries. I've needed operations since I've been here.

Q What would you like to do in the future?

A I would like to work here. I am good with computers and I would really like to study writing software. I already have approached a college to begin learning and then I hope to learn properly what I think I will be good at.

Q Do you think it is hard for people to understand what has happened in your life?

A Some people don't find it easy to believe how bad other people's lives can be. I don't feel comfortable when I am around them. They have no understanding of anything that is different from what they know in their lives. They cannot imagine how difficult it is to live in a country where corruption is normal.

Q Who has helped you most?

A A centre that helps asylum seekers and some individuals. Strangely enough one particular worker, the co-ordinator, is Greek and I was afraid to go to him at first because the Greeks and the Turks are ancient enemies - but he has been so very kind and helpful to me! Found me English classes, gave me food, he helped me a lot and he still helps me.

Q Do you have a girlfriend here?

A I did have an Australian-born girlfriend but her parents are Turkish and they recently took her back to Turkey where she became engaged. She is Muslim. (I am nominally Muslim but I am not a believer.) We really wanted to marry each other but I have nothing to offer her. I have nothing behind me so I felt I could not say anything. I feel very sad about this - but what can I do?

Q Is it hard to stop thinking about the past?

A Sometimes I have dreams - bad dreams, nightmares about the past and I wake up frightened. I feel I am falling. This happens often. But I try not to get depressed and to look forward to things. I also try to be active and involved here. If you just sit about the house all day it will certainly make you depressed and unhappy because you will only think about yourself. I still work for an activist movement for human rights here in Australia because it is so important that people understand and know about things.

Q What is frustrating to you?

A I would like you to understand me. I can't say all the right things, things that are very complex and painful. I want to say much more than this but the language isn't right. I would very much like real understanding. My life and thoughts are complex but as yet I have not the language to convey this. ■

> "Some people don't find it easy to believe how bad other people's lives can be."

Talking Points

◆ Tarik does not think Turkey is a democratic country. Why?

◆ Tarik was working for 'human rights' in Turkey. What do you understand by this term? Do you think these rights are worth the struggles that Tarik has been through?

◆ Tarik misses his family and friends, his country and also feels frustrated that he struggles to communicate his feelings in English and make new friends. What would be the most difficult problem for you, if you were in his situation?

Useful addresses and contacts

There are many organisations worldwide who work to assist and protect refugees. Here are just a few of them. The international websites can all be read in English.

International Organisation for Migration (IOM)
Works with migrants and governments to provide humane responses to migration.

17 Route des Morillons
CH-1211, Geneva 19,
Switzerland
www.iom.int

United Nations (UN)
An organisation that aims to promote international peace, develop friendly relations and promote a respect for human rights and freedoms.

Headquarters:
First Avenue at 46th Street
New York, NY 10017
www.un.org

United Nations High Commissioner for Refugees (UNHCR)
A branch of the UN that deals specifically with refugees.

Case Postale 2500, CH-1211,
Geneva 2, Switzerland
www.unhcr.ch

Refugee Council
Provides support and advice for refugees and asylum seekers.

Head office in UK:
240-250 Ferndale Road
London SW9 8BB
www.refugeecouncil.org.uk

Head office in Australia:
PO Box 946, Glebe, 2037,
Australia NSW 2037
www.refugeecouncil.org.au

European Council on Refugees and Exiles
An umbrella organisation of 72 refugee-assisting agencies in 28 countries.

ECRE Secretariat
103 Worship Street
London EC2A 2DF
www.ecre.org

National Immigration Forum
Promotes public policies in the USA that welcome immigrants and refugees.

50 F Street NW, Suite 300,
Washington DC 2000
www.immigrationforum.org

US Committee for Refugees
Defends the human rights of refugees and asylum seekers.

1717 Massachusetts Avenue
NW, 2nd Fl
Washington DC 20036
www.refugees.org

Amnesty International
Works to protect human rights worldwide.

UK:
The Human Rights Action Centre, 17-25 New Inn Yard
London EC2A 3EA

Australia:
Locked Bag 23, Broadway,
NSW 2007, Australia
www.amnesty.org

Glossary

asylum A special legal immigration status given to people who are recognised as refugees according to the 1951 UN convention on refugees.

asylum appeal If an asylum application is rejected, asylum seekers can appeal to have the decision overturned.

asylum seeker Someone seeking a special legal status called asylum or refugee status to stay in another country because they would be persecuted at home.

burka A long tent-like veil that covers women from head to foot. The Taliban movement in Afghanistan enforced a strict dress code that required Muslim women to wear a burka in public.

communism A way of governing a country, with all property publicly owned. Often communist governments are not elected by the people.

democracy A way of governing a country, with people elected to put forward the views of the people. Usually most property is owned privately.

DSS Department of Social Security in the UK.

Hazaras A minority ethnic group in Afghanistan who speak an archaic Persian. They are minority Shi'ites (followers of Shi'a Islam) within a dominant Sunni Muslim population.

Home Office The British government department that handles immigration.

Kalashnikov A type of rifle which originated in the USSR.

Koran The holy book of Islam.

Kosovo Liberation Army (KLA) An ethnic Albanian group that formed in the mid-1990s to seek independence for Kosovo. The KLA attacked Serbian police repeatedly from late 1997 to early 1998.

Molotov cocktail A small and basic bomb, usually made from a bottle filled with inflammable liquid.

mujahedin A group of fighters in an Islamic country, often following strict Islamic rules.

Nationalist (Romania) A person who wants the country for ethnic Romanians only.

NATO (North Atlantic Treaty Organisation) NATO began as a military association of European and North American states, formed in 1949 to defend Europe and the North Atlantic, mainly as a precaution against the Soviet Union. In the 1990s with the collapse of Communism in Eastern Europe and with concerns about Yugoslavia and some of the former Soviet republics, NATO began to take on a new role - that of peacekeeper and crisis manager.

Northern Alliance A group who fought against Taliban rule in Afghanistan. They contributed to the Taliban's overthrow in 2001.

Pashtuns The largest ethnic group in Afghanistan. The Pashtuns speak Pashtu, which is an Indo-Iranian language and one of the two official languages of Afghanistan.

racketeer A person who runs a dishonest business.

refugee Someone who has fled a country to seek asylum elsewhere and has been accepted as a refugee under international law because he or she has a well-founded fear of persecution.

Taliban A group that came to power in Afghanistan in 1996 after fierce fighting with the USSR and civil war. It imposed a strict Islamic regime on the country and was driven from power in 2001.

Uzbeks Ethnic group in Afghanistan who speak the Uzbek, a Turkic language.

visa A stamp on a passport to show that its bearer has been given permission to visit a country by embassy officials from the country.

welfare benefits Money given to people who are on low incomes, do not have access to decent housing, are suffering from illness or are unemployed.

Index

Getting active!

On your own:
Write a statement explaining your views about whether people coming to your country should be given refugee status or not. Explain your reasons and do some more research using local media.

In pairs:
Research an organisation that campaigns for and /or assists asylum seekers and refugees.

In groups:
Organise and tape a live TV-style debate about whether asylum seekers should be allowed to stay in the country. Some people could take the part of asylum seekers, perhaps using some of the interviews in the book to provide them with profiles. Organise people to take both sides of the arguement and conclude with an audience vote on the issue.